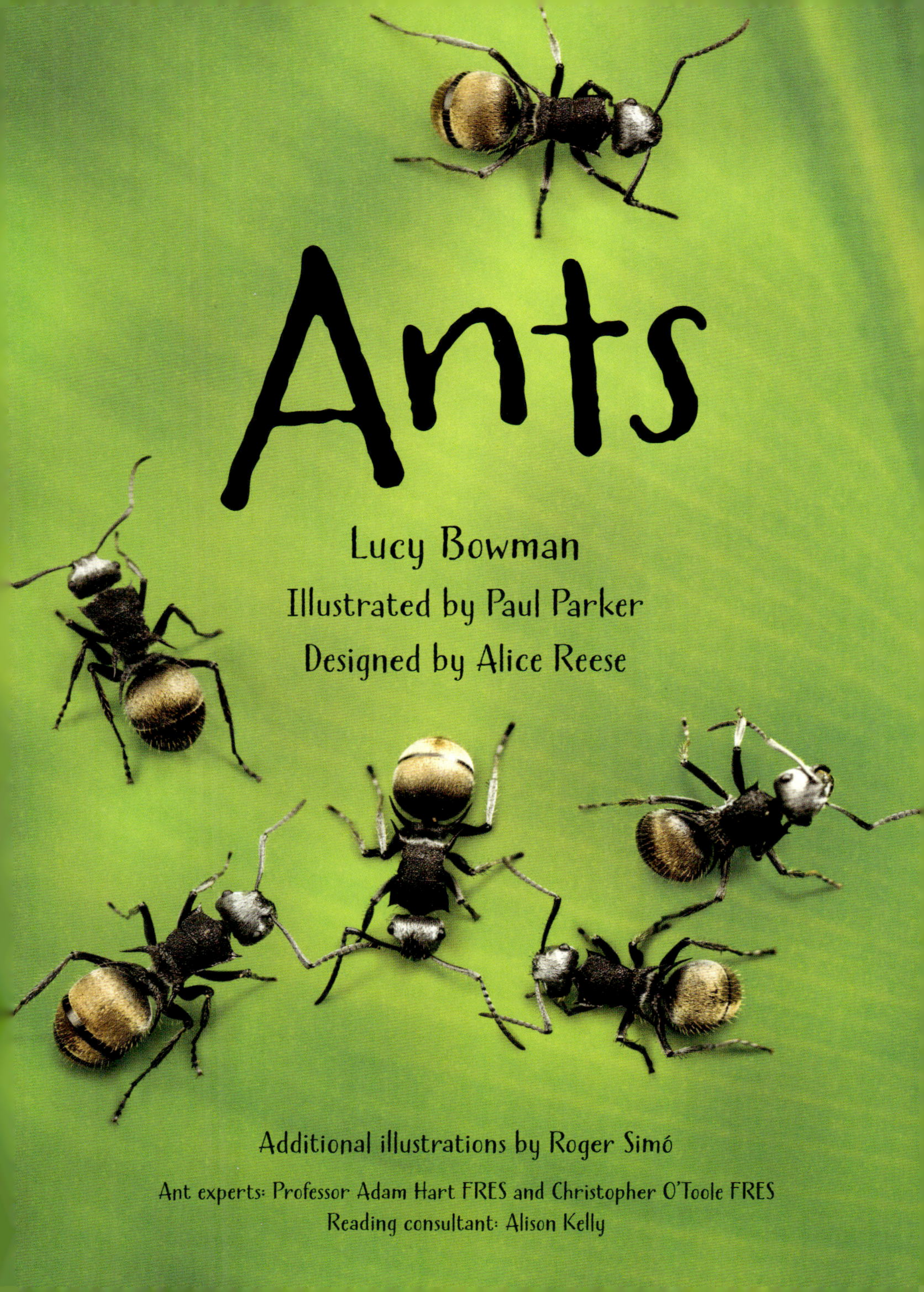

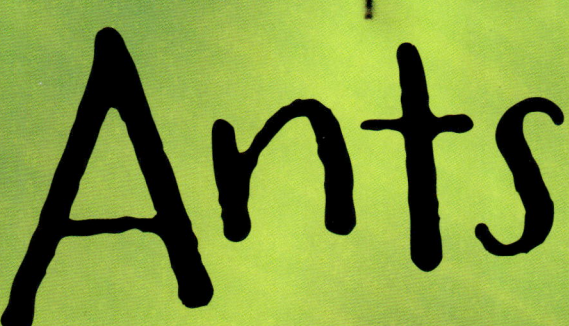

Ants

Lucy Bowman

Illustrated by Paul Parker

Designed by Alice Reese

Additional illustrations by Roger Simó

Ant experts: Professor Adam Hart FRES and Christopher O'Toole FRES
Reading consultant: Alison Kelly

Contents

- 3 Ant life
- 4 Close up
- 6 Busy ants
- 8 Building nests
- 10 Keeping safe
- 12 Under attack
- 14 Growing up
- 16 Starting a colony
- 18 Finding food
- 20 Growing fungus
- 22 Ants and aphids
- 24 Amazing ants
- 26 On the move
- 28 Desert ants
- 30 Glossary
- 31 Websites to visit
- 32 Index

Ant life

Ants are a type of insect. They live in nearly every country in the world.

Like all ants, these red harvester ants live and work together in a large group.

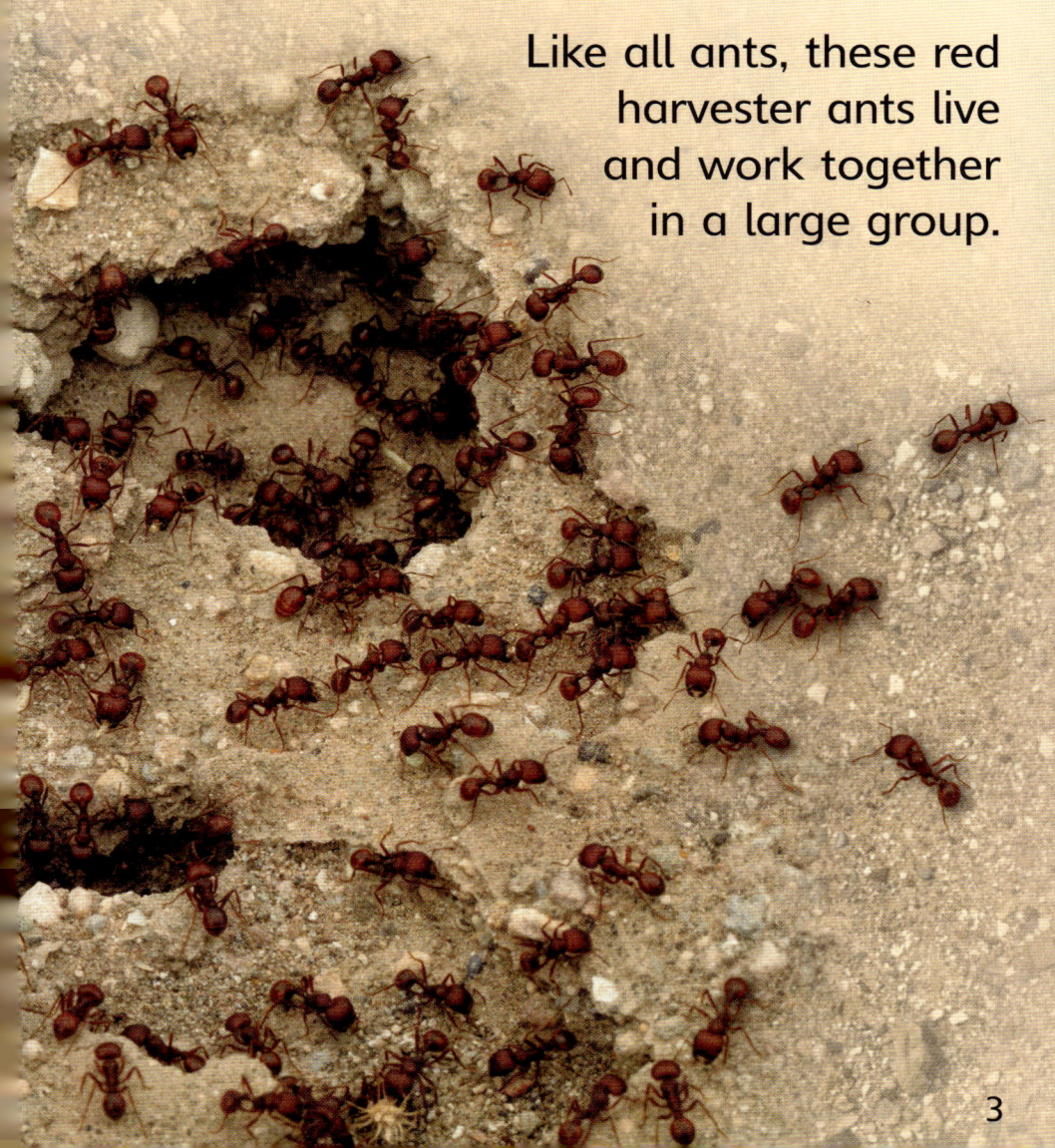

Close up

Ants have six legs. Their bodies are made of three main parts.

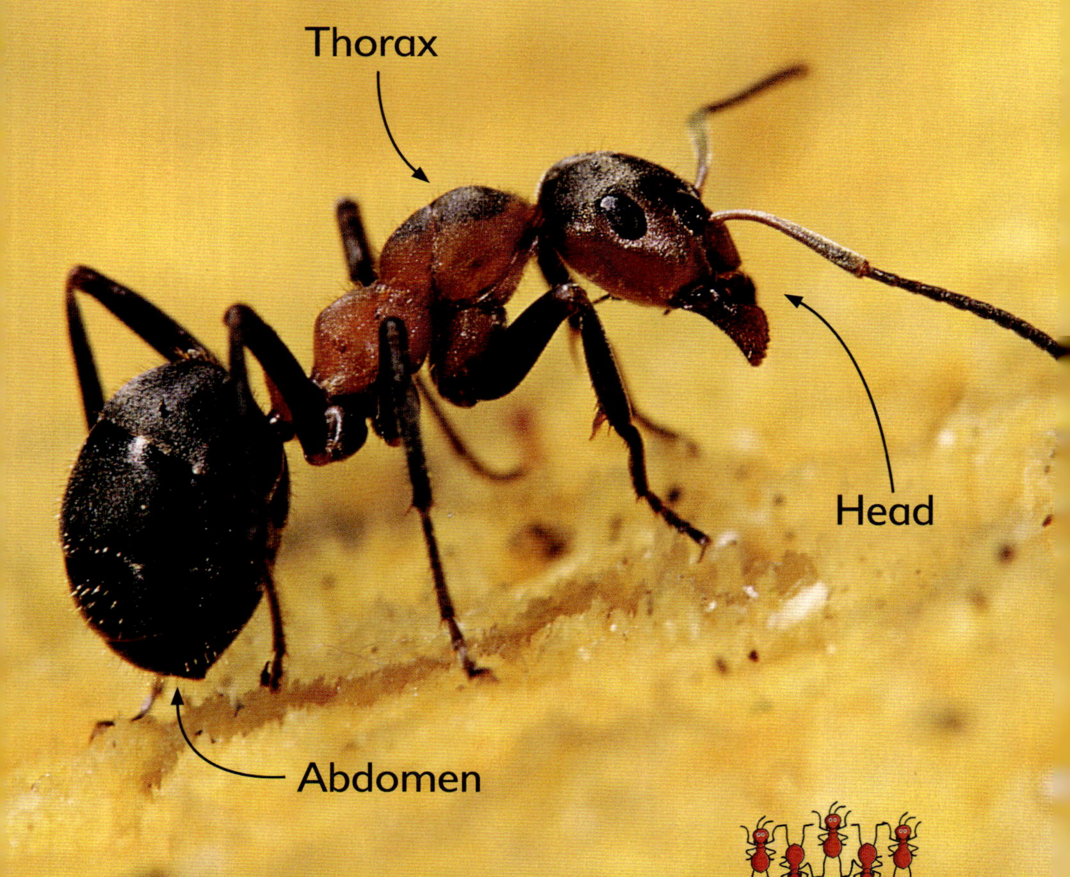

Thorax

Head

Abdomen

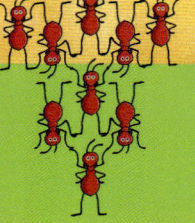

A single ant is strong enough to carry 50 ants.

Ants have feelers on their heads. They use them to touch and smell things.

They have strong jaws that they use to dig, cut, carry and protect themselves.

Their legs have hook-like claws that they use to climb plants.

They can even walk upside-down.

Busy ants

Ants live together in huge groups called colonies. The ants in a colony all have different jobs to do.

The queen is the mother of all the ants in the colony. She lays lots of eggs.

Worker ants take care of the other ants and bring food to them.

Some types of colonies have soldier ants. They fight off attackers.

This soldier ant has huge jaws.

It uses them to attack its enemies and to chop up large pieces of food.

Some queen ants can lay thousands of eggs in one day.

Building nests

Most ants live in nests. The nests can be different shapes and sizes.

Wood ants gather dead leaves and twigs and make a mound.

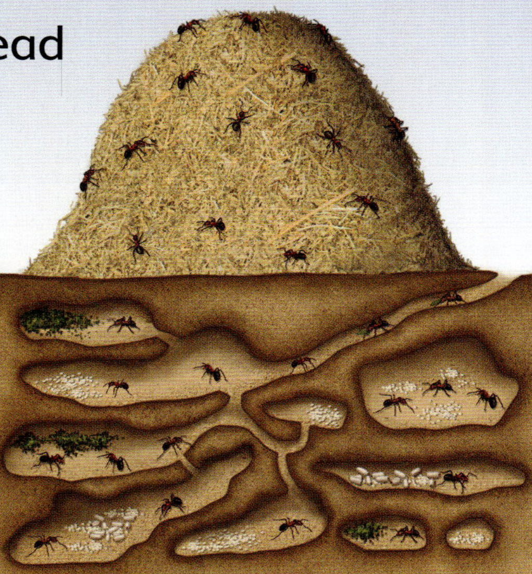

They build their nest by digging rooms and tunnels underneath.

If the nest is cold, ants sit in the sun and then go inside. Their bodies warm the nest.

If the nest gets hot, they dig holes in the mound so cool air can get in.

These weaver ants have made a nest from leaves glued together with sticky silk.

Some tiny ants make their nests inside acorns.

Keeping safe

Ants have clever ways of protecting themselves and their nests.

Turtle ants have wide heads that they use to stop attackers from getting into their nest.

These red wood ants are squirting smelly liquid.

The smell scares attackers away from the nest.

Bull ants inject an attacker with poison from the end of their abdomens.

A black carpenter ant explodes, covering its attacker in sticky glue so it can't move.

Bullet ants have the most painful sting in the world.

Under attack

There are many different creatures that eat ants for food.

A black bear and her cubs find an ant nest under a rock.

She uses her strong paws to flip the rock over.

The cubs lick up the ants and their young with their tongues.

Young insects known as antlions dig holes and eat any ants that fall into them.

This anteater has found an ant nest in a tree trunk.

It licks up lots of ants quickly, before they start to attack.

Growing up

Young ants hatch from eggs laid by a queen. They grow into adults in stages.

The eggs hatch and larvae come out. Adult ants care for them and feed them.

Each larva spins a silk shell called a cocoon, around itself. Its body changes inside.

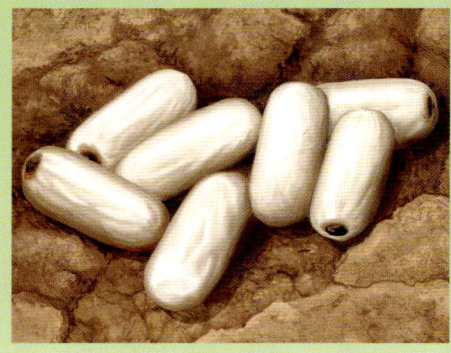

Around three weeks later, adult ants break out of the cocoons.

These ants are keeping their larvae clean to make sure they stay healthy.

Some ants grow up into adult ants without a cocoon.

Starting a colony

Some types of ants have wings. They fly away from their nest to start new colonies of their own.

A male and female carpenter ant fly into the air. Then they mate.

The female is now a queen. Her wings fall off. She finds a hole in an old log.

She lays lots of eggs. They grow into workers. This is the start of a new colony.

This carpenter ant worker is chewing wood away to make the nest hole bigger.

Some queens lick their eggs to make them hatch.

Finding food

Different types of ants eat different food, such as plants and other insects. The ants in a colony work together to collect food.

An ant finds seeds. As it goes back to its nest, it makes a smell that stays on the path.

Other ants from the colony follow the smell to find the seeds.

Each ant uses its strong jaws to carry a seed back to the nest.

These ants have found a dead centipede to eat.

They are helping each other carry it back to their nest.

Fire ants sometimes kill and eat small lizards.

Growing fungus

Fungus grows in some ant nests. The adult ants look after the fungus and feed it to their young.

Leafcutter ants bite off parts of the fungus and feed them to their larvae.

The ants also chew up leaves and push them into the fungus. This helps it to grow.

The ants take care of the fungus by keeping it clean and healthy.

This photo shows fungus growing inside the nest of some leafcutter ants.

 A young queen takes a piece of fungus to grow in her new nest.

Ants and aphids

Some ants feed on other creatures, without killing them.

Aphids are tiny insects. They suck sugary liquid from plants for food.

A liquid called honeydew leaks out of the back of their bodies.

Honeydew is a good ant food. Ants collect it and take it back to their nest.

Some ants take care of aphids, so they can collect honeydew all the time.

These ants are guarding aphids to keep any attackers away.

Sometimes ants take aphids to their nest to keep them safe.

Amazing ants

Ants can do incredible things.

This is a honeypot ant. It has stored food in its body, until it is so full that it can't move.

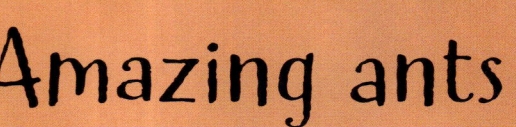

When other ants in the colony need food, the honeypot will spit some out.

Gliding ants can travel by gliding through the air.

Dracula ants drink their larvae's blood, without killing them.

Fire ants can float on water if they link their legs together to make a raft.

On the move

Army ants don't live in nests. Instead, they spend most of their lives moving from place to place.

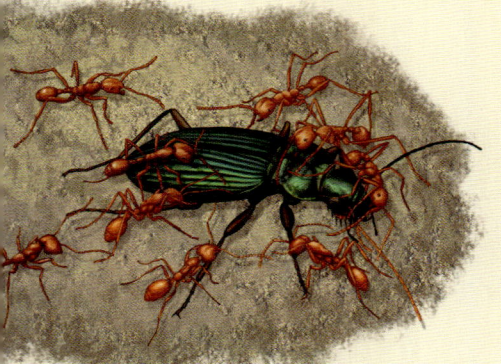

As they travel, they catch insects for food in their sharp, powerful jaws.

When the queen needs to lay eggs, all the ants stop until the eggs hatch.

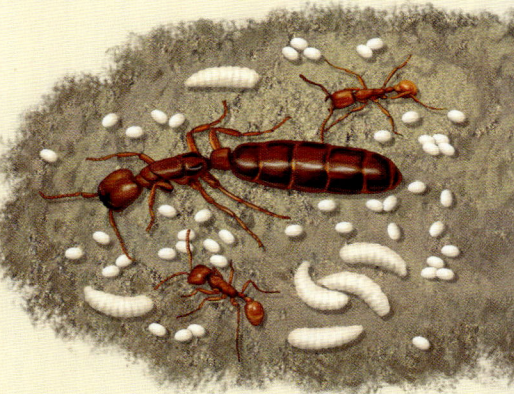

Then, the ants move off again. Workers carry and feed the larvae.

At night, the ants stand close together to make a shelter with their bodies.

The queen and her young are safe inside.

Army ants are usually blind. They use touch and smell to find their food.

Desert ants

Some ants can survive in extremely hot places, such as the Sahara Desert.

Silver ants dig a nest in the sand. It is cooler there than in the hot sun.

They stay in the nest until it is so hot that any attackers will have gone away.

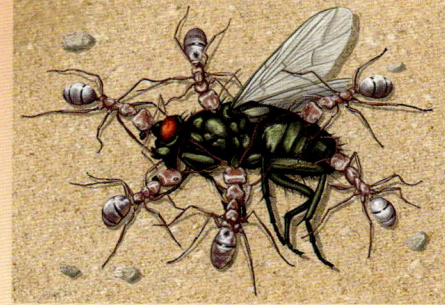

The silver ants are safe to leave their nest. They spread out looking for food.

They carry the food back to their nest quickly, before they become too hot.

Silver ants have very long legs that keep their bodies high off the hot sand.

Their bodies look shiny, because they are covered in tiny silver hairs.

Silver ants' hairs bounce back the sun's hot rays, helping the ants to stay cool.

Glossary

Here are some of the words in this book you might not know. This page tells you what they mean.

 thorax - the middle part of an ant's body.

 abdomen - the back part of an ant's body.

 feelers - parts on an ant's head that they use to touch and smell things.

 colony - a big group of ants that lives and works together.

 larva - an ant that's just hatched. When there are lots, they're called larvae.

 cocoon - a case that some larvae spin, before they become adults.

 fungus - related to mushrooms, it grows in some ant nests.

Websites to visit

You can visit exciting websites to find out more about ants. For links to sites with video clips and activities, go to the Usborne Quicklinks website at **www.usborne.com/quicklinks** and type in the keywords **"beginners ants"**.

Always ask an adult before using the internet and make sure you follow these basic rules:

1. Never give out personal information, such as your name, address, school or telephone number.

2. If a website asks you to type in your name or email address, check with an adult first.

The websites are regularly reviewed and the links at Usborne Quicklinks are updated. However, Usborne Publishing is not responsible and does not accept liability for the content or availability of any website other than its own. We recommend that children are supervised while on the internet.

These leafcutter ants are carrying leaf pieces back to their nest.

Index

abdomen, 4, 11, 30
aphids, 22-23
cocoon, 14, 15, 30
colonies, 6, 16, 18, 24, 30
digging, 5, 8, 28
eggs, 6, 7, 14, 16, 17, 26
feelers, 5
food, 6, 7, 12-13, 18-19, 20-21, 22, 23, 24, 25, 26, 27, 28
fungus, 20-21, 30
honeydew, 22, 23
jaws, 5, 7, 18, 26
larvae, 14-15, 20, 25, 26, 30
legs, 4, 5, 25, 29
nests, 8-9, 10, 12, 13, 16, 17, 18, 19, 20, 21, 22, 23, 26, 28
poison, 11
queens, 6, 7, 14, 16, 17, 21, 26, 27
silk, 9, 14
smelling, 5, 10, 18, 27
soldier ants, 6, 7
stinging, 11
thorax, 4
wings, 16
worker ants, 6, 16, 17, 26

Acknowledgments

Photographic manipulation by John Russell
Picture research by Ruth King

Photo credits

The publishers are grateful to the following for permission to reproduce material: cover © **Tim Flach/Getty Images**; p1© **alex wild/Alexander Wild**; p2-3 © **Don Johnston/All Canada Photos/SuperStock**; p4 © **Juniors/Juniors/SuperStock**; p5 © **Chua Wee Boo/age fotostock/SuperStock**; p6 © **alex wild/Alexander Wild**; p7 © **Adrian Hepworth/Alamy**; p9 © **Ingo Arndt/Getty Images**; p10-11 © **Kim Taylor/naturepl.com**; p13 © **John Cancalosi/ardea.com**; p15 © **Visuals Unlimited/naturepl.com**; p17 © **blickwinkel/Alamy**; p19 © **Diganta Talukdar/Demotix/Corbis**; p21 © **Mark Moffett/Minden Pictures/FLPA**; p23 © **Arterra Picture Library/Alamy**; p24 © **John Cancalosi/Getty Images**; p25 © **Nathan Mlot and David Hu, Georgia Tech**; p27 © **42-56243317/Minden Pictures/Corbis**; p29 © **Vincent Amouroux, Mona Lisa Production/Science Photo Library**; p31 © **Redmond Durrell/Alamy**.

Every effort has been made to trace and acknowledge ownership of copyright. If any rights have been omitted, the publishers offer to rectify this in any subsequent editions following notification.

First published in 2016 by Usborne Publishing Ltd., Usborne House, 83-85 Saffron Hill, London EC1N 8RT, England. www.usborne.com Copyright © 2016 Usborne Publishing Ltd. The name Usborne and the devices ♀☉ are Trade Marks of Usborne Publishing Ltd. All rights reserved. No part of this publication may be reproduced, stored in a retrieval system, or transmitted in any form or by any means, electronic, mechanical, photocopying, recording or otherwise without the prior permission of the publisher.
First published in America 2016. U.E.